Do You

Want to Be

A Social

Worker?

Information for student wanting to go into the

Social Work Field-from a Social Worker's point of

view

By

Samuel S. Smith, MHS, BA, LSW, CSW

Dedication

This book is dedicated to my Loving wife- Pamela Smith. She has been with me from our time we met while I was a Machine Gunner in the Marines. We had a rough first year with be discharge early from the Marines and having to be on Food stamps, healthy start gives you another prospection of life, and why we should not judges others you never know when you may need help. She pushed; support and I received an associate degree than went on for my bachelor degree and in 2010 receiving my Master's degree in Human Services. This goes out to my two Daughters- Samantha and Holly, and finally yet importantly in memory of my favorite woman of all time my mom Kathleen Frances Smith (Strickler).

Chapter 1

Some Fields of Social Work

The Social Work field has many great fields you can work in such has **Children Protective Service (CPS),** this field you will learn how to investigate allegations of abuse or neglect and emotional abuse. This field is a very high burn out rate due to the pressures of the job. If this is the area, you want to work in, you need to be very organized, and flexible most CPS jobs require on-call and removal of children from homes or having the alleged perpetrator to leave the home. You will work with many community resources to name a few the local police, court system, hospitals, and local schools. Has a CPS worker you will want to help everyone but it is the judge who makes the decisions of where a child is placed in foster or with another family or if child goes back to there home. The degree for this job is a bachelor degree in social work or related field.

Adult Protective Service (APS) in this field you are helping the elderly with alleged abuse such as physical abuse, neglect, financial issues. When we get old and need our family to care for us, they do not always do it for the right reasons. You will investigated to ensure the elderly are not being abuse or someone misusing there money. You will help elderly who have no family and may need to go to nursing home or an assistive living. In this position, you will work with many community resources to name a few the local police, court system, Nursing homes, assistive living, and hospitals. The degree for this job is a bachelor degree in social work or related field.

Nursing Homes in this field of Social Work your number one priority is to ensure that the resident's rights are being met at the nursing home. You will be counseling residents on give and take due to most residents share a room one wants it hot one wants it cold or other little things that come up. You are also there for the staff and helping them with advice on situations, such has when residents pass away, they have been caring for the residents, and sometimes this is very hard on the staff and yourself. When working in this field you need to learn how to accept this part of the job.

You will learn how to care plan for patient, complete MDS and have weekly conferences for skilled patients, help with admissions, counsel the residents when issues occur and usually you will have a case load of 100 residents if the nursing is bigger than 100 they will have another social worker in the building. You will also doing discharge planning for your skilled patient who are just there for rehab they may need services such as home health, Medical equipment, or go to an assistive living. The degree for this job is a Bachelor degree.

Hospital in this field you are Case Management/Discharge Planner or Medical Social

Worker. You will arrange patient's discharges at home with home health or set up rehab in skilled nursing home (SNF). Complete Pasrr's and Fl-2. Help with linking patients to community resources. You have the conflict of the patient may need to be in the hospital longer but the insurance is not paying so you have to discharge the patient. You talk with patients and family to set up discharge arrangements and sometime patient do not get to go where they want for rehab due to no beds or other issues that may come up. You cannot choose or recommend where patient goes for therapy or placement. You have to give them a list of your community resources and let them choose, you send out referrals to all your (skilled nursing facilities), or SNF is if they are Medicare or Medicaid. Private insurances is different they contract with SNF's and not all SNF's take private insurances. There are many rules in discharging patients to SNF's and you have to learn about Medicare and Medicaid guidelines. Some on call may be required depending on the hospital.

This is a fast pace job and must be organized and work well with others. You will work with most of the hospital staff has a discharge planner and will need to know your community resources well. You will need a Master degree in Social Work or Bachelor degree in Social Work with experience. These jobs is now called case management and switch to be done by RN's due to the insurance piece to discharge planning,

Hospice Social Worker is a wonderful field of Social Work most of Hospice agencies are a team of nursing, pastors, doctor, volunteers, and social worker. The Social Worker, can do the following run the Bereavement Groups and make bereavement visits & make Social Work visits for Home Health. Counseled family and children about end of life concerns they may have and help prepare for patients death such as having them choose a funeral home and get everything in order and preparing them of what is coming. There is also fund raising with many of your Hospice Agencies to help the patients that cannot pay for the Hospice services. You will need a Master degree in Social Work or Bachelor degree in Social Work with experience.

IN North Carolina there is a grant program called-**Community Alterative Program for**

Disabled Adults (CAP/DA) and Children with medical disabilities. This program is ran by the local hospital, Department of Social Services or Senior Services. The one I worked for was through local hospital in the Home Health in this field you will have a caseload 30 and up. You make home visits each monthly, & make Social Work visits for Home Health. There is a lot of paperwork for this job you complete assessments, complete fl-2s, ensure the in-home–aides are working when they should be working. Ensuring patient stays within set budget for equipment and in-home care. This program is different in each state but for you will need a Bachelor degree in Social Work.

Mental Health field of Social Work these social workers are in high demand and many states do not have the resources need to help this population. In the field you will do some counseling and find appropriate placement if need. The clients with drug and alcohol issue fall under this umbrella along with your mental health clients with little resources for your clients this is a hard field to work in but worth it when you can get them help and they want the help. You will need a Master degree in Social Work or Bachelor degree in Social Work with experience.

Homeless field of Social Work is ran by your local shelter such as the Salvation Army or church groups that they also provide help with finding housing, jobs, meals. They usually run the soup kitchens for the community, this is a wonderful field, and everyone should take the time to volunteer at the soup kitchen. The Soup Kitchen are mostly all volunteers but for the a few paid staff, for the counseling of clients. Senior Services will have meals for seniors and have the program Meal on Wheels that are delivered to the elderly in need.

Veteran Service Offices is another area of Social Work you help veterans in need for receiving the disability from service connect injuries to just helping with rent, food or sometime home equipment like wheelchair ramps. They help get set up in the VA medical system and transport you to the hospitals if needed or to local clinics.

There are many more fields you have choose to from these are some of the areas that I have worked in over my years of being a Social Worker.

Chapter 2

Personal Experience

My Social Work Career began due I was discharged from the Marines from having serve heat stroke I was newly married and my wife was 6 months pregnant. Thankful I was referred to Veteran Service Offices of my county while in College and the Veteran service officer is the one that help me get my VA benefits and get this degree in Social Work.

From a career test at the VA and it stated what your interest was I really wanted to be a Math teacher, but they pick Social Work, due to Social Work had a two year-degree, and go on for a four-year degree. My high school grades were not the best so I had to prove I could get this degree. The program was great it paid for by books, college, and I received money to live on with my wife and child at home.

To give back for the help we received, I completed one of my free internship with the Veteran Service Office.

When going to school for Social Work I did my internship at Adult Protective Service (APS). The one case that I remember was when I went out with the APS worker who has worked in this field a long time the old man was at the door with a shotgun in his hand I thought I served the Marines and me going to be shot here. The Social Work said the man's name and told put the gun down I here to give you your weekly allowance and he did put down the gun. I did not know that the people in the area have robbed the man so that why he had a gun. The Social Work had establish a good relationship with her client and that it the key when you have long-term clients.

Working in the Mental Health was my first job as a Social Worker it was a nursing home but we had mental health patient due to state cutbacks. I started out as an Activities Director and went on to be Social Worker. When first start I had a two degree in Social Work and went back for my four-year degree while working full-time. I had a ward of 40 woman, I was in charge of that had all of the mental illness you can name, but it was a great learning experience for me to know what medications help want mental health illness. This job helped me pass my LSW exam due to the experience I learned with these residents.

When I worked in nursing homes, it is nice
for a social worker who is at the end of their career
it is more paperwork and same thing every day at a
Nursing Homes. In this field, you will be more like
a mediator between the residents. You talk with
residents about who should be able to have the TV
on and when to have the TV off in the shared room.
The unforgettable care plan that was required. I had
a couple that was long-term residents and they want
to have sexual relationship. I had to set this care
plan up and the staff hated me for it, but it was there
wright. I had to have the MD write a note that the
residents were medically safe for this and then I had
to set a time for this to happen, but you could not
have signs on the room. The staff that was directly
working with these residents were informed by
myself or charge nurse, when the residents were

going to have their together time. What I like about
working in the nursing home is this is these
residents home and you are their guest like spending
time with them learning about their experiences and
meeting their families. The hard part about the
nursing home is when families just drop off the love
one and never come and see them. These would be
the patients I would take some time with and visit
with them. The nursing homes now are changing
and most now have a skilled wing for short-term
patients who just need rehab and then go home this
makes the job more appealing to a younger social
worker due to they are help with the discharge
needs and setting up service for when these resident
go back home. The skilled side of nursing homes is
how they make money for the long-term side to stay
open.

When working in Children Protective Service (CPS) the first thing is the cases or calls that come in are Alleged Abuse, which means you do not know if the child was abused or not so when going to investigate allegations of abuse or neglect, sexual and emotional abuse. You gather your facts from all sides ensuring the safety of the child and or self at times and then based of the facts you determine the outcome. Do not assume that all reports are true. I have had many Custody cases that people call in so they can get custody of child when the child was fine you need to be very detailed at this job and not become judgmental.

This field is a very high burn out rate due to the pressures of the job and the case loads of workers. When working for a sexual abuse unit in a big city I had a caseload of 30 child sexual cases

and you had to investigate and either close them or

refer them to the ongoing service within 30 days

you received the report. You can request from

supervisor for a 15-day extension if you have good

cause such as waiting for police reports or hospital

test.

When working in this field you take those

children that you help and that family that you were

able to get them back together with their parent

after they have had help and completed their case

plan. The most rewarding felling for me today is

that I help a child that did not go back with his

family but had to place in residential treatment due

to he would not follow the rules in foster care. The

child received is GED in the residential treatment

and went on to college and now this child is and

Adult and has a college degree and is doing great.

When working for the CAP/DA Program it
was great due to you help the elderly stay in their
own home with family and they do not have to go
into a nursing home. I loved visiting my patient
monthly and ensuring there needs was being met by
the services that I set up for them. I enjoyed
spending time with them in their home and learning
about their families and work life. It was hard when
a patient was no longer safe to be home and they
had to go into nursing home but at least they were
able to stay home for a time.

I wanted to worker for Hospice due to my
mother pass away from cancer and wanted to be a

part of the field it was very rewarding but for social work only so much to do as the social worker sometime this is part-time position depending on how big of an agency you work for. This was hard time for me to work in this field but I was able to relate with families that lost a love one and ran the Bereavement Groups and make bereavement visits & make Social Work visits for Home Health. This was best part of the job.

Working in the hospital setting came last in my Social Work career. This job is very fast pace and all about get people out of hospital as soon as they were ready for discharge and setting them up with outside services or making referrals for them. Help with linking patients to community resources. What I did not like in this job, was the part of having the conflict of the patient may need to be in the hospital longer but the insurance is not paying so you have to discharge the patient. You talk with patients and family to set up discharge arrangements and sometime patient do not get to go where they want for rehab due to no beds or other issues that may come up. You cannot choose or recommend where patient goes for therapy or placement. You have to give them a list of your community resources and let them choose, you send out referrals to all your (skilled nursing facilities), or SNF's if they are Medicare or Medicaid. Private insurances is different they contract with SNF's and not all SNF's take private insurances. There are many rules in discharging patients to SNF's and you have to learn about Medicare and Medicaid guidelines. Some on call may be required depending on the hospital. I for see this job is now being taken over by RN's due to the insurance piece to discharge planning I for see this job ending for Social Workers.

Chapter 3

Tips on How to Cope

How I coped in the field of Social Work is change before burn out happens, leave work life at work and your home life at home. This sound easy but it is hard for some people I have always been able to complete this part due to Social Work is very confidential and you cannot talk about your job like working at some regular jobs. The field of Social Work has many different jobs you can do and if you get to appoint where you cannot take it anymore, change to another field of social work. This will make you a better social worker. The more experiences you have the better social worker you will be from the experience of more than just one field of social work. Do not be afraid of making some mistakes and you will make them we all do. Just learn from them so you do not make that mistake again. We may not be able to help everyone in social work field but there will always be a couple of clients, you helped whether you know it or not. Talk with your co-worker they are social workers and understand what you are going through. This field is not for everyone some people think they can save everyone this is not the case.

You can only help someone, when their ready for the help. This is very true for people with addition to something until they are ready to get help you, cannot force it they will not follow through. When dealing with a person-yelling let them get off their chest do not tell them to calm down it will just be worse. Usually they are fine and then will talk with you if not leave and come back later after they calm down you cannot argue with someone that is mad. Remember the field of Social Work is getting bigger by the years, and there are many fields to work. If one field does not work, try another field as you see I have worked in many fields of Social Work and glad that I had a chance to work with all the wonderful co-workers and patients, client, and residents.

Chapter 4

Is it for you?

I remember my first Social Work course and I walked into the room it was all women in the room. I thought I had the wrong class but the professor at the time, a female I might add, stated welcome to the class. This field is like nursing a female dominate field. We need more strong males in the field of Social Work for the young males who need a good role model. Some fields of Social Work can be dangerous like in the bigger cities doing CPS cases and mental health field at times.

If you like working with people and truly want to help others help themselves than this is for you.   This is not a job you will get rich at even though I have a Master Degree my wife with a Two-year Nursing degree make more money than I do. You do not get into social work for the pay. This is a very thankless jobs at time the social work is not always people favorite word to here they think you are there to take their child or place there love one in a nursing home. If you are a person who needs to be praise for a good job, this might not be the job for you. There are times were you get the praise and this is great hold on to those moments.

To be a Social Worker is to be here for your clients, patients, families, and residents and to ensure they get the respect and dignity they deserve. You treat all people how you want to be treated. You are not here to judge people, but to help them get through a tough time in their lives.

This has been the best career I have had, and to think I did not even know what a Social Worker was until the VA choose this career for me.

In closing, I hope this book helps you know a little about the social work field and if you really want to be a Social Worker.

About the Author

I have work as a Social Worker for 19 years; I am LSW in Ohio, and CSW in North Carolina.

I have a MS in Human Services and BA in Social Work.

www.ingramcontent.com/pod-product-compliance
Lightning Source LLC
Chambersburg PA
CBHW070258300526
45791CB00022B/1635